Especially for

_____

From

_____

Date

_____

Published by Barbour Publishing, Inc., P.O. Box 719, Uhrichsville, Ohio 44683, www.barbourbooks.com

Our mission is to publish and distribute inspirational products offering exceptional value and biblical encouragement to the masses.

Member of the
Evangelical Christian
Publishers Association

Printed in China.

365 Promises
for Women

BARBOUR
PUBLISHING

January 1

Create in me a clean heart, O God; and renew a right spirit within me. Cast me not away from thy presence; and take not thy holy spirit from me. Restore unto me the joy of thy salvation; and uphold me with thy free spirit.

PSALM 51:10–12 KJV

January 2

The sun will no more be your light by day, nor will the brightness of the moon shine on you, for the LORD will be your everlasting light, and your God will be your glory. Your sun will never set again, and your moon will wane no more; the LORD will be your everlasting light.

ISAIAH 60:19–20 NIV

December 31

I close my letter with these last words: Rejoice. . . .
Encourage each other. Live in harmony and peace.
Then the God of love and peace will be with you.

2 CORINTHIANS 13:11 NLT

January 3

Isn't everything you have and everything you are sheer gifts
from God? . . . You already have all you need.

1 CORINTHIANS 4:7–8 MSG

December 30

Whether you turn to the right or to the left, your ears will hear a voice behind you, saying, "This is the way; walk in it."

ISAIAH 30:21 NIV

January 4

Go ye therefore, and teach all nations. . .teaching them to observe all things whatsoever I have commanded you: and, lo, I am with you alway, even unto the end of the world.

MATTHEW 28:19–20 KJV

December 29

So spacious is [Christ], so roomy, that everything of God finds its proper place in him without crowding. Not only that, but all the broken and dislocated pieces of the universe—people and things, animals and atoms—get properly fixed and fit together in vibrant harmonies.

COLOSSIANS 1:19–20 MSG

January 5

For no matter how many promises God has made, they
are "Yes" in Christ. And so through him the "Amen"
is spoken by us to the glory of God.

2 CORINTHIANS 1:20 NIV

December 28

Lo, the star, which they saw in the east, went before
them, till it came and stood over where the young
child was. . . . And when they were come into
the house, they saw the young child with Mary
his mother, and fell down, and worshipped him.

MATTHEW 2:9, 11 KJV

January 6

"Do not worry about your life, what you will eat, or about your body, what you will wear. For life is more than food, and the body more than clothing. Consider the ravens: they neither sow nor reap, they have neither storehouse nor barn, and yet God feeds them. Of how much more value are you than the birds!"

LUKE 12:22–24 NRSV

December 27

Thanks be unto God for his unspeakable gift.

2 CORINTHIANS 9:15 KJV

January 7

"My Presence will go with you, and I will give you rest."

EXODUS 33:14 NIV

December 26

At once the angel was joined by a huge angelic choir singing
God's praises: "Glory to God in the heavenly heights, peace
to all men and women on earth who please him."

LUKE 2:13–14 MSG

January 8

Show me your ways, O LORD, teach me your paths; guide me in your truth and teach me, for you are God my Savior, and my hope is in you all day long. Remember, O LORD, your great mercy and love, for they are from of old.

PSALM 25:4–6 NIV

December 25

Behold, a virgin shall be with child, and shall bring forth a son, and they shall call his name Emmanuel. . .God with us.

MATTHEW 1:23 KJV

January 9

So, chosen by God for this new life of love, dress in the wardrobe God picked out for you: compassion, kindness, humility, quiet strength, discipline. . . . And regardless of what else you put on, wear love. It's your basic, all-purpose garment. Never be without it.

COLOSSIANS 3:12–14 MSG

December 24

For to us a child is born, to us a son is given, and
the government will be on his shoulders. And
he will be called Wonderful Counselor, Mighty God,
Everlasting Father, Prince of Peace.

Isaiah 9:6 niv

January 10

Your promises have been thoroughly tested;
that is why I love them so much.

PSALM 119:140 NLT

December 23

And the Word was made flesh, and dwelt among us,
(and we beheld his glory, the glory as of the only
begotten of the Father,) full of grace and truth.

JOHN 1:14 KJV

January 11

Two are better than one, because they have a good reward for their toil. For if they fall, one will lift up the other; but woe to one who is alone and falls and does not have another to help.

ECCLESIASTES 4:9–10 NRSV

December 22

But when the right time came, God sent his Son, born of a woman, subject to the law. God sent him to buy freedom for us who were slaves to the law, so that he could adopt us as his very own children.

GALATIANS 4:4–5 NLT

January 12

There is no room in love for fear. Well-formed love banishes fear. Since fear is crippling, a fearful life—fear of death, fear of judgment—is one not yet fully formed in love.

1 JOHN 4:18 MSG

December 21

For you know the grace of our Lord Jesus Christ, that
though he was rich, yet for your sakes he became poor, so
that you through his poverty might become rich.

2 CORINTHIANS 8:9 NIV

January 13

Mercy, peace and love be yours in abundance.

JUDE 1:2 NIV

December 20

"Because of the tender mercy of our God. . .the rising sun
will come to us from heaven to shine on those living in
darkness and in the shadow of death, to guide
our feet into the path of peace."

LUKE 1:78–79 NIV

God is sheer mercy and grace; not easily angered, he's rich in love. . . . He doesn't treat us as our sins deserve, nor pay us back in full for our wrongs. As high as heaven is over the earth, so strong is his love to those who fear him. And as far as sunrise is from sunset, he has separated us from our sins.

PSALM 103:8, 10–12 MSG

December 19

Surely your goodness and unfailing love will pursue
me all the days of my life, and I will live
in the house of the LORD forever.

PSALM 23:6 NLT

January 15

Prepare your minds for action; be self-controlled;
set your hope fully on the grace to be given
you when Jesus Christ is revealed.

1 PETER 1:13 NIV

December 18

Your love, O LORD, reaches to the heavens,
your faithfulness to the skies.

PSALM 36:5 NIV

January 16

Thus says the LORD: Do not let the wise boast in their wisdom, do not let the mighty boast in their might, do not let the wealthy boast in their wealth; but let those who boast boast in this, that they understand and know me, that I am the LORD; I act with steadfast love, justice, and righteousness in the earth, for in these things I delight.

JEREMIAH 9:23–24 NRSV

December 17

Love mixed with faith be yours from God the Father and from the Master, Jesus Christ. Pure grace and nothing but grace be with all who love our Master, Jesus Christ.

EPHESIANS 6:23–24 MSG

January 17

"It's who you are and the way you live that count before God. Your worship must engage your spirit in the pursuit of truth. That's the kind of people the Father is out looking for: those who are simply and honestly themselves before him in their worship. God is sheer being itself—Spirit. Those who worship him must do it out of their very being, their spirits, their true selves, in adoration."

JOHN 4:23–24 MSG

December 16

The LORD will keep you from all harm—he will watch over your life; the LORD will watch over your coming and going both now and forevermore.

PSALM 121:7–8 NIV

January 18

He will yet fill your mouth with laughter
and your lips with shouts of joy.

JOB 8:21 NIV

December 15

The righteous cry out, and the LORD hears them; he delivers them from all their troubles. The LORD is close to the brokenhearted and saves those who are crushed in spirit.

PSALM 34:17–18 NIV

January 19

Have mercy on me, O God, according to your unfailing love; according to your great compassion blot out my transgressions. . . . Wash me, and I will be whiter than snow.

PSALM 51:1, 7 NIV

December 14

GOD, your God, will cut away the thick calluses
on your heart and your children's hearts,
freeing you to love GOD, your God, with your
whole heart and soul and live, really live.

DEUTERONOMY 30:6 MSG

January 20

"I will make my people strong with power from me!
They will go wherever they wish, and wherever
they go, they will be under my personal care."

ZECHARIAH 10:12 TLB

December 13

Above all else, guard your heart,
for it is the wellspring of life.

PROVERBS 4:23 NIV

January 21

The Lord is in his holy temple; the Lord's throne
is in heaven. His eyes behold, his gaze examines
humankind. . . . For the Lord is righteous; he loves
righteous deeds; the upright shall behold his face.

Psalm 11:4, 7 nrsv

December 12

And God raised us up with Christ and seated us with him
in the heavenly realms in Christ Jesus, in order that in the
coming ages he might show the incomparable riches of his
grace, expressed in his kindness to us in Christ Jesus.

EPHESIANS 2:6–7 NIV

January 22

"But I lavish my love on those who love me and obey my commands, even for a thousand generations."

DEUTERONOMY 5:10 NLT

December 11

Whom have I in heaven but you? And earth has nothing I desire besides you. My flesh and my heart may fail, but God is the strength of my heart and my portion forever.

PSALM 73:25–26 NIV

January 23

And I heard, as it were, the voice of a great multitude and as
the sound of many waters and as the sound of mighty peals
of thunder, saying, "Hallelujah! For the Lord our God, the
Almighty, reigns. Let us rejoice and be glad and give
the glory to Him, for the marriage of the Lamb has
come and His bride has made herself ready."

REVELATION 19:6–7 NASB

December 10

No one has ever seen God. But if we love each other, God lives in us, and his love has been brought to full expression through us.

1 JOHN 4:12 NLT

January 24

Open your mouth and taste, open your eyes and see—
how good GOD is. Blessed are you who run to him.
Worship GOD if you want the best; worship
opens doors to all his goodness.

PSALM 34:8–9 MSG

December 9

The angel of the LORD encamps around
those who fear him, and he delivers them.

PSALM 34:7 NIV

January 25

At that time I will make a treaty. . . . I will bind you to me forever with chains of righteousness and justice and love and mercy. I will betroth you to me in faithfulness and love, and you will really know me then as you never have before.

HOSEA 2:18–20 TLB

December 8

LORD, walking in the way of your laws, we wait
for you; your name and renown are the desire of
our hearts. My soul yearns for you in the night;
in the morning my spirit longs for you.

ISAIAH 26:8–9 NIV

January 26

The LORD bless thee, and keep thee: The LORD make his face shine upon thee, and be gracious unto thee: The LORD lift up his countenance upon thee, and give thee peace.

NUMBERS 6:24–26 KJV

December 7

The Lord is my strength and my shield;
my heart trusts in him, and I am helped.

PSALM 28:7 NIV

January 27

The deeper your love, the higher it goes; every cloud is
a flag to your faithfulness. Soar high in the skies,
O God! Cover the whole earth with your glory!

PSALM 57:10–11 MSG

December 6

What marvelous love the Father has extended
to us! Just look at it—we're called children
of God! That's who we really are.

1 JOHN 3:1 MSG

January 28

May the LORD, the God of your ancestors, increase you a thousand times more and bless you, as he has promised you!

DEUTERONOMY 1:11 NRSV

December 5

"Be still, and know that I am God; I will be exalted
among the nations, I will be exalted in the earth."

PSALM 46:10 NIV

January 29

Because of Christ and our faith in him, we can now come fearlessly into God's presence, assured of his glad welcome.

EPHESIANS 3:12 NLT

December 4

And he said, Go forth, and stand upon the mount before the LORD. And, behold, the LORD passed by, and a great and strong wind rent the mountains. . .but the LORD was not in the wind: and after the wind an earthquake; but the LORD was not in the earthquake: And after the earthquake a fire; but the LORD was not in the fire: and after the fire a still small voice. And it was so.

1 KINGS 19:11–13 KJV

January 30

May our Lord Jesus Christ himself and God our Father, who loved us and by his grace gave us eternal encouragement and good hope, encourage your hearts and strengthen you in every good deed and word.

2 THESSALONIANS 2:16–17 NIV

December 3

He heals the heartbroken and bandages their wounds.
He counts the stars and assigns each a name.
Our Lord is great, with limitless strength; we'll
never comprehend what he knows and does.

PSALM 147:3–5 MSG

January 31

Love never gives up, never loses faith, is always hopeful, and
endures through every circumstance. Love will last forever.

1 Corinthians 13:7–8 nlt

December 2

Carry each other's burdens, and in this
way you will fulfill the law of Christ.

GALATIANS 6:2 NIV

February 1

You also were included in Christ when you heard the word of truth, the gospel of your salvation. Having believed, you were marked in him with a seal, the promised Holy Spirit.

EPHESIANS 1:13 NIV

December 1

Those who are gentle and lowly will possess the land; they will live in prosperous security.

PSALM 37:11 NLT

February 2

Encourage one another daily, as long as it is called
today. . . . We have come to share in Christ if we
hold firmly till the end the confidence we had at first.

HEBREWS 3:13–14 NIV

November 30

Therefore be imitators of God, as beloved
children, and live in love, as Christ loved us.

EPHESIANS 5:1–2 NRSV

February 3

Not to us, O Lord, not to us, but to your name give glory,
for the sake of your steadfast love and your faithfulness.

PSALM 115:1 NRSV

November 29

The LORD is my shepherd, I shall not want. He makes me lie down in green pastures; he leads me beside still waters; he restores my soul. He leads me in right paths for his name's sake. Even though I walk through the darkest valley, I fear no evil; for you are with me; your rod and your staff—they comfort me.

PSALM 23:1–4 NRSV

February 4

With the Lord a day is like a thousand years, and a
thousand years are like a day. The Lord is not slow in
keeping his promise, as some understand slowness. He is
patient with you, not wanting anyone to perish,
but everyone to come to repentance.

2 PETER 3:8–9 NIV

November 28

Yet the LORD longs to be gracious to you; he rises
to show you compassion. For the LORD is a God
of justice. Blessed are all who wait for him!

ISAIAH 30:18 NIV

February 5

I look behind me and you're there, then up ahead and you're there, too—your reassuring presence, coming and going. This is too much, too wonderful—I can't take it all in!

PSALM 139:5–6 MSG

November 27

Give thanks to the LORD, for he is good. His love
endures forever. Give thanks to the God of gods.
His love endures forever. Give thanks to the lord of lords:
His love endures forever. To him who alone does
great wonders, His love endures forever.

PSALM 136:1–4 NIV

February 6

For everything that was written in the past was written
to teach us, so that through endurance and the
encouragement of the Scriptures we might have hope.

ROMANS 15:4 NIV

November 26

"For you will go out with joy, and be led forth with peace;
the mountains and the hills will break forth into
shouts of joy before you, and all the trees
of the field will clap their hands."

ISAIAH 55:12 NASB

February 7

Confess your sins to one another, and pray for one
another, so that you may be healed. The prayer
of the righteous is powerful and effective.

JAMES 5:16 NRSV

November 25

The steadfast love of the LORD never ceases, his mercies never come to an end; they are new every morning; great is your faithfulness.

LAMENTATIONS 3:22–23 NRSV

February 8

Jesus. . .said to them, "Let the little children come to me; do not stop them; for it is to such as these that the kingdom of God belongs."

MARK 10:14 NRSV

November 24

All praise to the God and Father of our
Lord Jesus Christ. He is the source of every mercy
and the God who comforts us. He comforts us in all
our troubles so that we can comfort others.

2 CORINTHIANS 1:3–4 NLT

February 9

But seek ye first the kingdom of God, and his
righteousness; and all these things shall be added unto you.

MATTHEW 6:33 KJV

November 23

O LORD, you are my God; I will exalt you and praise
your name, for in perfect faithfulness you have
done marvelous things, things planned long ago.

ISAIAH 25:1 NIV

February 10

GOD made my life complete when I placed all the pieces before him. When I got my act together, he gave me a fresh start. . . . GOD rewrote the text of my life when I opened the book of my heart to his eyes.

PSALM 18:20, 24 MSG

November 22

The LORD is gracious, and full of compassion;
slow to anger, and of great mercy.

PSALM 145:8 KJV

February 11

"For I know the plans I have for you," declares the LORD, "plans to prosper you and not to harm you, plans to give you hope and a future."

JEREMIAH 29:11 NIV

November 21

But thanks be to God, who always leads us in triumphal
procession in Christ and through us spreads everywhere
the fragrance of the knowledge of him. For we
are to God the aroma of Christ among those who
are being saved and those who are perishing.

2 CORINTHIANS 2:14–15 NIV

"The joy of the LORD is your strength!"

NEHEMIAH 8:10 NLT

November 20

Enter his gates with thanksgiving and his courts
with praise; give thanks to him and praise his name.

PSALM 100:4 NIV

February 13

When I consider thy heavens, the work of thy fingers,
the moon and the stars, which thou hast ordained;
What is man, that thou art mindful of him? and the son
of man, that thou visitest him? For thou hast made
him a little lower than the angels, and hast
crowned him with glory and honour.

PSALM 8:3–5 KJV

November 19

Give thanks to the LORD, for he is good!
His faithful love endures forever.

1 CHRONICLES 16:34 NLT

February 14

Love is patient, love is kind. It does not envy, it does not boast, it is not proud. It is not rude, it is not self-seeking, it is not easily angered, it keeps no record of wrongs. Love does not delight in evil but rejoices with the truth.

1 CORINTHIANS 13:4–6 NIV

November 18

Now that we know what we have—Jesus, this great High Priest with ready access to God—let's not let it slip through our fingers. We don't have a priest who is out of touch with our reality. He's been through weakness and testing, experienced it all—all but the sin. So let's walk right up to him and get what he is so ready to give. Take the mercy, accept the help.

HEBREWS 4:14–16 MSG

February 15

Yes, because GOD's your refuge, the High God your very own home, evil can't get close to you, harm can't get through the door. He ordered his angels to guard you wherever you go.

PSALM 91:9–11 MSG

November 17

Holy, holy, holy, is the LORD of hosts:
the whole earth is full of his glory.

ISAIAH 6:3 KJV

February 16

Pure gold put in the fire comes out of it proved
pure; genuine faith put through this suffering comes
out proved genuine. When Jesus wraps this all
up, it's your faith, not your gold, that God will
have on display as evidence of his victory.

1 PETER 1:7 MSG

November 16

"It is good to proclaim your unfailing love in the morning, your faithfulness in the evening."

PSALM 92:2 NLT

February 17

May the God of hope fill you with all joy and peace
as you trust in him, so that you may overflow with
hope by the power of the Holy Spirit.

ROMANS 15:13 NIV

November 15

"I am the Vine, you are the branches. When you're joined with me and I with you, the relation intimate and organic, the harvest is sure to be abundant."

JOHN 15:5 MSG

He is like a father to us, tender and sympathetic to those who reverence him. For he knows we are but dust, and that our days are few and brief, like grass, like flowers.

PSALM 103:13–15 TLB

November 14

I sought the LORD, and he answered me; he delivered me from all my fears. Those who look to him are radiant; their faces are never covered with shame.

PSALM 34:4–5 NIV

February 19

Praise be to the God and Father of our Lord Jesus Christ,
who has blessed us in the heavenly realms with
every spiritual blessing in Christ. For he chose us
in him before the creation of the world to
be holy and blameless in his sight.

EPHESIANS 1:3–4 NIV

November 13

"Fear not, for I have redeemed you; I have summoned you by name; you are mine. When you pass through the waters, I will be with you; and when you pass through the rivers, they will not sweep over you. When you walk through the fire, you will not be burned; the flames will not set you ablaze."

ISAIAH 43:1–2 NIV

February 20

"By this everyone will know that you are my disciples, if you have love for one another."

JOHN 13:35 NRSV

November 12

His huge outstretched arms protect you—under them
you're perfectly safe; his arms fend off all harm. . . .
No harm will even graze you. You'll stand
untouched, watch it all from a distance.

PSALM 91:4, 7–8 MSG

February 21

You give them drink from your river of delights.
For with you is the fountain of life; in your light we see light.

PSALM 36:8–9 NIV

November 11

Finally, beloved, whatever is true, whatever is honorable, whatever is just, whatever is pure, whatever is pleasing, whatever is commendable, if there is any excellence and if there is anything worthy of praise, think about these things.

PHILIPPIANS 4:8 NRSV

February 22

Whither thou goest, I will go; and where thou lodgest, I will lodge: thy people shall be my people, and thy God my God.

RUTH 1:16 KJV

November 10

For God is sheer beauty, all-generous
in love, loyal always and ever.

PSALM 100:5 MSG

February 23

For the LORD takes delight in his people; he crowns the humble with salvation. Let the saints rejoice in this honor and sing for joy.

PSALM 149:4–5 NIV

November 9

My heart took delight in all my work, and
this was the reward for all my labor.

ECCLESIASTES 2:10 NIV

February 24

These commandments that I give you today are to be upon your hearts. Impress them on your children. Talk about them when you sit at home and when you walk along the road, when you lie down and when you get up.

DEUTERONOMY 6:6–7 NIV

November 8

My frame was not hidden from you when I was made
in the secret place. When I was woven together in
the depths of the earth, your eyes saw my unformed
body. All the days ordained for me were written
in your book before one of them came to be.

PSALM 139:15–16 NIV

We're depending on GOD; he's everything we need.
What's more, our hearts brim with joy since we've taken
for our own his holy name. Love us, GOD, with all
you've got—that's what we're depending on.

PSALM 33:20–22 MSG

November 7

He wants not only us but everyone saved, you know,
everyone to get to know the truth we've learned: that there's
one God and only one, and one Priest-Mediator between
God and us—Jesus, who offered himself in exchange for
everyone held captive by sin, to set them all free.

1 TIMOTHY 2:4–6 MSG

February 26

Honor and majesty are before him; strength
and beauty are in his sanctuary.

PSALM 96:6 NRSV

November 6

"Loose the chains of injustice and untie the cords of the
yoke, to set the oppressed free and break every yoke. . . .
Then your light will break forth like the dawn, and
your healing will quickly appear; then your
righteousness will go before you, and the glory of
the LORD will be your rear guard."

ISAIAH 58:6, 8 NIV

February 27

God is able to make all grace abound to you, so
that in all things at all times, having all that you
need, you will abound in every good work.

2 CORINTHIANS 9:8 NIV

November 5

Since God assured us, "I'll never let you down, never walk off and leave you," we can boldly quote, "God is there, ready to help; I'm fearless no matter what. Who or what can get to me?"

HEBREWS 13:5–6 MSG

He didn't tiptoe around God's promise asking cautiously skeptical questions. He plunged into the promise and came up strong, ready for God, sure that God would make good on what he had said. That's why it is said, "Abraham was declared fit before God by trusting God to set him right." But it's not just Abraham; it's also us! The same thing gets said about us when we embrace and believe the One who brought Jesus to life.

ROMANS 4:20–24 MSG

November 4

If my people, which are called by my name, shall humble themselves, and pray, and seek my face, and turn from their wicked ways; then will I hear from heaven, and will forgive their sin, and will heal their land.

2 CHRONICLES 7:14 KJV

March 1

"Worship the Lord your God and only the Lord your God.
Serve him with absolute single-heartedness."

LUKE 4:8 MSG

November 3

I thank my God every time I remember you. In all my prayers for all of you, I always pray with joy.

PHILIPPIANS 1:3–4 NIV

March 2

In his unfailing love, my God will come and help me.

PSALM 59:10 NLT

November 2

I wait for the LORD, my soul waits, and in his word
I put my hope. My soul waits for the LORD more
than watchmen wait for the morning, more
than watchmen wait for the morning.

PSALM 130:5–6 NIV

March 3

"I will pour out my Spirit on all people. Your sons and daughters will prophesy, your old men will dream dreams, your young men will see visions. Even on my servants, both men and women, I will pour out my Spirit in those days. I will show wonders in the heavens and on the earth."

JOEL 2:28–30 NIV

November 1

If you give, you will receive. Your gift will return to you
in full measure, pressed down, shaken together to
make room for more, and running over. Whatever
measure you use in giving—large or small—it will
be used to measure what is given back to you.

LUKE 6:38 NLT

March 4

With my whole heart have I sought thee: O let me not wander from thy commandments. Thy word have I hid in mine heart, that I might not sin against thee. . . . I will delight myself in thy statutes: I will not forget thy word.

PSALM 119:10–16 KJV

October 31

And this same God who takes care of me will
supply all your needs from his glorious riches,
which have been given to us in Christ Jesus.

PHILIPPIANS 4:19 NLT

March 5

The LORD. . .is righteous; he does no wrong.
Morning by morning he dispenses his justice,
and every new day he does not fail.

ZEPHANIAH 3:5 NIV

October 30

Now God, don't hold out on me, don't hold
back your passion. Your love and truth
are all that keeps me together.

PSALM 40:11 MSG

March 6

O how abundant is your goodness that you have laid up
for those who fear you, and accomplished for those
who take refuge in you, in the sight of everyone!

PSALM 31:19 NRSV

Don't worry about anything; instead, pray about everything. Tell God what you need, and thank him for all he has done.

PHILIPPIANS 4:6 NLT

March 7

We throw open our doors to God and discover at the same moment that he has already thrown open his door to us. We find ourselves standing where we always hoped we might stand—out in the wide open spaces of God's grace and glory, standing tall and shouting our praise.

ROMANS 5:2 MSG

October 28

The LORD is slow to anger and great in power; the LORD will
not leave the guilty unpunished. His way is in the whirlwind
and the storm, and clouds are the dust of his feet.

NAHUM 1:3 NIV

March 8

"You have made known to me the paths of life;
you will fill me with joy in your presence."

ACTS 2:28 NIV

October 27

You have not come to a mountain that can be touched. . . .
But you have come to Mount Zion, to the heavenly
Jerusalem, the city of the living God. You have come to
thousands upon thousands of angels in joyful assembly,
to the church of the firstborn, whose names are written
in heaven. You have come to God, the judge of all
men. . .to Jesus the mediator of a new covenant.

HEBREWS 12:18, 22–24 NIV

March 9

God's Spirit is right alongside helping us along. If we don't
know how or what to pray, it doesn't matter. He does our
praying in and for us, making prayer out of our wordless
sighs, our aching groans. He knows us far better than we
know ourselves. . .and keeps us present before God.
That's why we can be so sure that every detail in our lives
of love for God is worked into something good.

ROMANS 8:26–28 MSG

October 26

We all live off his generous bounty, gift after gift after gift. . . . This exuberant giving and receiving, this endless knowing and understanding—all this came through Jesus, the Messiah.

JOHN 1:16–17 MSG

March 10

Blessed are the peacemakers: for they
shall be called the children of God.

MATTHEW 5:9 KJV

October 25

O LORD, our Lord, how majestic is your name in all the
earth! You have set your glory above the heavens.

PSALM 8:1 NIV

March 11

I say to myself, "The LORD is my portion; therefore I will wait for him." The LORD is good to those whose hope is in him, to the one who seeks him; it is good to wait quietly for the salvation of the LORD.

LAMENTATIONS 3:24–26 NIV

October 24

Jesus said, "I am the Bread of Life. The person who aligns
with me hungers no more and thirsts no more, ever. . . .
Whoever believes in me has real life, eternal life."

JOHN 6:35, 47 MSG

March 12

For you were going astray like sheep, but now you have returned to the shepherd and guardian of your souls.

1 PETER 2:25 NRSV

October 23

I will praise you, O Lord, with all my heart; I will tell of all your wonders. I will be glad and rejoice in you; I will sing praise to your name, O Most High.

PSALM 9:1–2 NIV

March 13

Wait on the LORD: be of good courage, and he shall strengthen thine heart: wait, I say, on the LORD.

PSALM 27:14 KJV

October 22

Humble yourselves therefore under the mighty hand of
God, that he may exalt you in due time: Casting all
your care upon him; for he careth for you.

1 PETER 5:6–7 KJV

March 14

But the fruit of the Spirit is love, joy, peace,
patience, kindness, goodness, faithfulness, gentleness
and self-control. Against such things there is no law.

GALATIANS 5:22–23 NIV

October 21

But he said to me, "My grace is sufficient for you,
for my power is made perfect in weakness."
Therefore I will boast all the more gladly about
my weaknesses, so that Christ's power may rest on me.

2 CORINTHIANS 12:9 NIV

March 15

I urge you to live a life worthy of the calling you
have received. Be completely humble and gentle;
be patient, bearing with one another in love.

EPHESIANS 4:1–2 NIV

October 20

It is more blessed to give than to receive.

ACTS 20:35 KJV

March 16

"But I'll take the hand of those who don't know the way, who can't see where they're going. I'll be a personal guide to them, directing them through unknown country. I'll be right there to show them what roads to take, make sure they don't fall into the ditch. These are the things I'll be doing for them—sticking with them, not leaving them for a minute."

ISAIAH 42:16 MSG

October 19

Trust in the LORD with all your heart and lean not on your own understanding; in all your ways acknowledge him, and he will make your paths straight.

PROVERBS 3:5–6 NIV

March 17

You've always been great toward me—what love!
You snatched me from the brink of disaster! . . . You,
O God, are both tender and kind, not easily angered,
immense in love, and you never, never quit.

PSALM 86:13, 15 MSG

October 18

"Praise be to the name of God for ever and ever; wisdom and power are his. He changes times and seasons; he sets up kings and deposes them. He gives wisdom to the wise and knowledge to the discerning. He reveals deep and hidden things; he knows what lies in darkness, and light dwells with him."

DANIEL 2:20–22 NIV

March 18

But we see Jesus, who was made a little lower than the
angels, now crowned with glory and honor because
he suffered death, so that by the grace of God
he might taste death for everyone.

HEBREWS 2:9 NIV

October 17

What a wildly wonderful world, GOD! You made it all,
with Wisdom at your side, made earth overflow with
your wonderful creations. . . . All the creatures look
expectantly to you. . . . The glory of GOD—let it
last forever! Let GOD enjoy his creation!

PSALM 104:24, 27, 31 MSG

March 19

Though the fig tree does not bud and there are no grapes on the vines, though the olive crop fails and the fields produce no food. . .yet I will rejoice in the LORD, I will be joyful in God my Savior.

HABAKKUK 3:17–18 NIV

October 16

Commit your work to the LORD, and
your plans will be established.

PROVERBS 16:3 NRSV

March 20

Everyone who has left houses or brothers or sisters or father or mother or children or fields, for my name's sake, will receive a hundredfold, and will inherit eternal life.

MATTHEW 19:29 NRSV

October 15

For my thoughts are not your thoughts, neither are your ways my ways, saith the LORD. For as the heavens are higher than the earth, so are my ways higher than your ways, and my thoughts than your thoughts.

ISAIAH 55:8–9 KJV

March 21

For, lo, the winter is past, the rain is over and
gone; the flowers appear on the earth; the
time of the singing of birds is come.

SONG OF SOLOMON 2:11–12 KJV

October 14

A friend loves at all times, and a
brother is born for adversity.

PROVERBS 17:17 NIV

March 22

For he will command his angels concerning you to guard
you in all your ways; they will lift you up in their hands,
so that you will not strike your foot against a stone.

PSALM 91:11–12 NIV

October 13

Thy word is a lamp unto my feet, and a light unto my path.

PSALM 119:105 KJV

March 23

Little children, let us love, not in word
or speech, but in truth and action.

1 JOHN 3:18 NRSV

October 12

I appeal to you therefore, brothers and sisters, by the
mercies of God, to present your bodies as a living sacrifice,
holy and acceptable to God, which is your spiritual worship.
Do not be conformed to this world, but be transformed by
the renewing of your minds, so that you may discern what is
the will of God—what is good and acceptable and perfect.

ROMANS 12:1–2 NRSV

March 24

But for you who revere my name, the sun of
righteousness will rise with healing in its wings.

MALACHI 4:2 NIV

LORD, you are our Father. We are the clay, and you are the potter. We are all formed by your hand.

ISAIAH 64:8 NLT

March 25

Give generously, for your gifts will return to you later.

ECCLESIASTES 11:1 NLT

October 10

You're my place of quiet retreat; I wait for your Word to renew me. . .therefore I lovingly embrace everything you say.

PSALM 119:114, 119 MSG

March 26

No test or temptation that comes your way is beyond the course of what others have had to face. All you need to remember is that God will never let you down; he'll never let you be pushed past your limit; he'll always be there to help you come through it.

1 Corinthians 10:13 MSG

October 9

Real wisdom, God's wisdom, begins with a holy life and is characterized by getting along with others. It is gentle and reasonable, overflowing with mercy and blessings, not hot one day and cold the next, not two-faced. You can develop a healthy, robust community that lives right with God and enjoy its results only if you do the hard work of getting along with each other, treating each other with dignity and honor.

JAMES 3:17–18 MSG

March 27

The steadfast love of the LORD is from everlasting
to everlasting on those who fear him, and his
righteousness to children's children.

PSALM 103:17 NRSV

October 8

"Be strong and courageous, do not be afraid or tremble. . .
for the LORD your GOD is the one who goes with
you. He will not fail you or forsake you."

DEUTERONOMY 31:6 NASB

March 28

Therefore, since we have been justified through faith,
we have peace with God through our Lord Jesus Christ,
through whom we have gained access by faith into
this grace in which we now stand. And we rejoice
in the hope of the glory of God.

ROMANS 5:1–2 NIV

October 7

"Humanly speaking, it is impossible. But not with God. Everything is possible with God."

MARK 10:27 NLT

March 29

Bless the LORD, O my soul, and do not forget all his benefits—who forgives all your iniquity, who heals all your diseases, who redeems your life from the Pit, who crowns you with steadfast love and mercy, who satisfies you with good as long as you live so that your youth is renewed like the eagle's.

PSALM 103:2–5 NRSV

October 6

The LORD leads with unfailing love and faithfulness
all those who keep his covenant and obey his decrees.

PSALM 25:10 NLT

March 30

Let us draw near to God with a sincere heart in full assurance of faith. . . . Let us hold unswervingly to the hope we profess, for he who promised is faithful. And let us consider how we may spur one another on toward love and good deeds. Let us not give up meeting together. . .but let us encourage one another—and all the more as you see the Day approaching.

HEBREWS 10:22–25 NIV

October 5

"For he is the living God and he endures forever; his kingdom will not be destroyed, his dominion will never end. He rescues and he saves; he performs signs and wonders in the heavens and on the earth."

DANIEL 6:26–27 NIV

March 31

Are not five sparrows sold for two pennies? Yet not one
of them is forgotten in God's sight. But even the hairs
of your head are all counted. Do not be afraid;
you are of more value than many sparrows.

LUKE 12:6–7 NRSV

October 4

Cast thy burden upon the LORD, and he shall sustain thee:
he shall never suffer the righteous to be moved.

PSALM 55:22 KJV

April 1

Surely he hath borne our griefs, and carried our sorrows: yet
we did esteem him stricken, smitten of God, and afflicted.
But he was wounded for our transgressions, he was
bruised for our iniquities: the chastisement of our peace
was upon him; and with his stripes we are healed.

Isaiah 53:4–5 KJV

October 3

The Spirit of the Sovereign LORD is on me, because the LORD has anointed me to preach good news to the poor. He has sent me to bind up the brokenhearted, to proclaim freedom for the captives and release from darkness for the prisoners.

ISAIAH 61:1 NIV

April 2

"I have told you these things, so that in me you may
have peace. In this world you will have trouble.
But take heart! I have overcome the world."

JOHN 16:33 NIV

October 2

Come, and let us go up to the mountain of the LORD. . .and he will teach us of his ways, and we will walk in his paths.

MICAH 4:2 KJV

April 3

Now upon the first day of the week, very early in the
morning, they came unto the sepulcher. . . . And they found
the stone rolled away from the sepulchre. And they
entered in, and found not the body of the Lord Jesus.
And. . .behold, two men stood by them in shining
garments: And as they were afraid, and bowed down their
faces to the earth, they said unto them, Why seek ye the
living among the dead? He is not here, but is risen.

LUKE 24:1–6 KJV

October 1

For in Him all the fulness of Deity dwells in bodily form,
and in Him you have been made complete, and He
is the head over all rule and authority.

COLOSSIANS 2:9–10 NASB

April 4

Ask rain from the LORD in the season of the spring rain, from the LORD who makes the storm clouds, who gives showers of rain to you, the vegetation in the field to everyone.

ZECHARIAH 10:1 NRSV

September 30

So be truly glad! There is wonderful joy ahead, even though
it is necessary for you to endure many trials for a while. . . .
You love him even though you have never seen him.
Though you do not see him, you trust him; and even now
you are happy with a glorious, inexpressible joy.

1 PETER 1:6, 8 NLT

April 5

The Spirit of the Lord GOD is upon me; because the LORD
hath anointed me. . .to comfort all that mourn. . .to give
unto them beauty for ashes, the oil of joy for mourning, the
garment of praise for the spirit of heaviness; that
they might be called trees of righteousness, the
planting of the LORD, that he might be glorified.

ISAIAH 61:1–3 KJV

September 29

For we are God's workmanship, created in Christ Jesus to do good works, which God prepared in advance for us to do.

EPHESIANS 2:10 NIV

April 6

Grace, mercy and peace from God the Father and from Jesus Christ, the Father's Son, will be with us in truth and love.

2 JOHN 1:3 NIV

September 28

All Scripture is inspired by God and profitable for teaching, for reproof, for correction, for training in righteousness.

2 TIMOTHY 3:16 NASB

April 7

We all, like sheep, have gone astray, each of us
has turned to his own way; and the LORD has
laid on him the iniquity of us all.

ISAIAH 53:6 NIV

September 27

The human mind plans the way, but
the LORD directs the steps.

PROVERBS 16:9 NRSV

April 8

For Christ's love compels us, because we are convinced that
one died for all, and therefore all died. And he died for all,
that those who live should no longer live for themselves
but for him who died for them and was raised again. . . .
Therefore, if anyone is in Christ, he is a new
creation; the old has gone, the new has come!

2 CORINTHIANS 5:14–15, 17 NIV

September 26

And now these three remain: faith, hope and
love. But the greatest of these is love.

1 Corinthians 13:13 NIV

April 9

Do not let this Book of the Law depart from your
mouth; meditate on it day and night, so that you may
be careful to do everything written in it.
Then you will be prosperous and successful.

JOSHUA 1:8 NIV

September 25

"Rejoice in the LORD your God, for he has given you the autumn rains in righteousness. He sends you abundant showers, both autumn and spring rains, as before. The threshing floors will be filled with grain; the vats will overflow with new wine and oil."

JOEL 2:23–24 NIV

April 10

"Don't be afraid, for I am with you. Do not be dismayed, for I am your God. I will strengthen you. I will help you. I will uphold you with my victorious right hand."

ISAIAH 41:10 NLT

September 24

For the word of God is living and active.
Sharper than any double-edged sword, it penetrates even to
dividing soul and spirit, joints and marrow; it judges
the thoughts and attitudes of the heart.

HEBREWS 4:12 NIV

April 11

This is the day which the LORD hath made;
we will rejoice and be glad in it.

PSALM 118:24 KJV

September 23

Prove me, O Lord, and try me; test my heart
and mind. For your steadfast love is before my
eyes, and I walk in faithfulness to you.

PSALM 26:2–3 NRSV

April 12

Because of his great love for us, God, who is rich in mercy, made us alive with Christ even when we were dead in transgressions. . . . For it is by grace you have been saved, through faith—and this not from yourselves, it is the gift of God—not by works, so that no one can boast.

EPHESIANS 2:4–5, 8–9 NIV

September 22

Joyfully you'll pull up buckets of water from the
wells of salvation. And as you do it, you'll say,
"Give thanks to GOD. Call out his name.
Ask him anything! Shout to the nations, tell them
what he's done, spread the news of his great reputation!

ISAIAH 12:3–4 MSG

April 13

He raised [Christ] from the dead and seated him at his right hand in the heavenly realms, far above all rule and authority, power and dominion, and every title that can be given, not only in the present age but also in the one to come.

EPHESIANS 1:20–21 NIV

September 21

To every thing there is a season, and a
time to every purpose under the heaven.

ECCLESIASTES 3:1 KJV

April 14

If I speak with the tongues of men and of angels, but do not have love, I have become a noisy gong or a clanging cymbal. And if I have the gift of prophecy, and know all mysteries and all knowledge; and if I have all faith, so as to remove mountains, but do not have love, I am nothing.

1 CORINTHIANS 13:1–2 NASB

September 20

Listen, I will tell you a mystery! We will not all die, but we will all be changed, in a moment, in the twinkling of an eye, at the last trumpet. For the trumpet will sound, and the dead will be raised imperishable, and we will be changed.

1 CORINTHIANS 15:51–52 NRSV

April 15

Ever since I heard about your faith in the Lord Jesus and
your love for all the saints, I have not stopped giving
thanks for you, remembering you in my prayers.
I keep asking that the God of our Lord Jesus Christ,
the glorious Father, may give you the Spirit of wisdom
and revelation, so that you may know him better.

EPHESIANS 1:15–17 NIV

September 19

"Have I not commanded you? Be strong and courageous!
Do not tremble or be dismayed, for the Lord
your God is with you wherever you go."

JOSHUA 1:9 NASB

April 16

I want to know Christ and the power of his resurrection and the fellowship of sharing in his sufferings, becoming like him in his death, and so, somehow, to attain to the resurrection from the dead. Not that I have already obtained all this, or have already been made perfect, but I press on to take hold of that for which Christ Jesus took hold of me.

PHILIPPIANS 3:10–12 NIV

September 18

"I am the gate; whoever enters through me will be saved."

JOHN 10:9 NIV

April 17

In love he predestined us to be adopted as his sons through Jesus Christ, in accordance with his pleasure and will—to the praise of his glorious grace, which he has freely given us in the One he loves.

Ephesians 1:4–6 niv

September 17

"Ask, and it shall be given to you; seek, and you shall find; knock, and it shall be opened to you. For everyone who asks, receives; and he who seeks, finds; and to him who knocks, it shall be opened."

LUKE 11:9–10 NASB

April 18

Draw close to God, and God will draw close to you.

JAMES 4:8 NLT

September 16

Love your enemies. Let them bring out the best in you, not
the worst. When someone gives you a hard time, respond
with the energies of prayer, for then you are working
out of your true selves, your God-created selves.
This is what God does. He gives his best—the sun
to warm and the rain to nourish—to everyone.

MATTHEW 5:44–45 MSG

April 19

May the Lord make your love increase and overflow for each
other and for everyone else, just as ours does for you.
May he strengthen your hearts so that you will be
blameless and holy in the presence of our God and
Father when our Lord Jesus comes with all his holy ones.

1 THESSALONIANS 3:12–13 NIV

September 15

Those who love me, I will deliver; I will protect those who know my name. When they call to me, I will answer them; I will be with them in trouble, I will rescue them and honor them.

PSALM 91:14–15 NRSV

April 20

I will love thee, O LORD, my strength. The LORD is my rock, and my fortress, and my deliverer; my God, my strength, in whom I will trust; my buckler, and the horn of my salvation, and my high tower. I will call upon the LORD, who is worthy to be praised: so shall I be saved from mine enemies.

PSALM 18:1–3 KJV

September 14

"Call to Me and I will answer you, and I will tell you great
and mighty things, which you do not know."

JEREMIAH 33:3 NASB

April 21

"Listen to me. . .you whom I have upheld since you were conceived, and have carried since your birth. Even to your old age and gray hairs I am he, I am he who will sustain you. I have made you and I will carry you."

ISAIAH 46:3–4 NIV

September 13

"He is not far from each one of us. 'For in him
we live and move and have our being.'"

ACTS 17:27–28 NIV

April 22

O the depth of the riches both of the wisdom and
knowledge of God! how unsearchable are his judgments,
and his ways past finding out! For who hath known the
mind of the Lord? or who hath been his counsellor?

ROMANS 11:33–34 KJV

September 12

I am the LORD, and there is no other; apart from me there is no God. I will strengthen you, though you have not acknowledged me, so that from the rising of the sun to the place of its setting men may know there is none besides me.

ISAIAH 45:5–6 NIV

April 23

"For as the rain and the snow come down from heaven, and do not return there without watering the earth. . .so shall My word be which goes forth from My mouth; it shall not return to Me empty, without accomplishing what I desire."

ISAIAH 55:10–11 NASB

September 11

When calamity comes, the wicked are brought
down, but even in death the righteous have a refuge.

PROVERBS 14:32 NIV

April 24

"You know with all your heart and soul that not one of all the good promises the LORD your God gave you has failed. Every promise has been fulfilled; not one has failed."

JOSHUA 23:14 NIV

September 10

Bless the LORD, O you his angels, you mighty ones
who do his bidding. . . . Bless the LORD, all his works,
in all places of his dominion. Bless the LORD, O my soul.

PSALM 103:20, 22 NRSV

April 25

I've learned by now to be quite content whatever my circumstances. I'm just as happy with little as with much, with much as with little. I've found the recipe for being happy whether full or hungry, hands full or hands empty. Whatever I have, wherever I am, I can make it through anything in the One who makes me who I am.

PHILIPPIANS 4:11–13 MSG

September 9

Jesus said to her, "Everyone who drinks of this water will be thirsty again, but those who drink of the water that I will give them will never be thirsty. The water that I will give will become in them a spring of water gushing up to eternal life."

JOHN 4:13–14 NRSV

April 26

"Remember the former things, those of long ago; I am God, and there is no other; I am God, and there is none like me. I make known the end from the beginning, from ancient times, what is still to come. I say: My purpose will stand, and I will do all that I please."

ISAIAH 46:9–10 NIV

September 8

Your Father already knows your needs. He will
give you all you need from day to day.

LUKE 12:30–31 NLT

April 27

"Whoever does the will of my Father in heaven is my brother and sister and mother."

MATTHEW 12:50 NIV

September 7

Delight yourself in the LORD and he will give you the desires of your heart. Commit your way to the LORD; trust in him and he will do this: He will make your righteousness shine like the dawn, the justice of your cause like the noonday sun.

PSALM 37:4–6 NIV

April 28

I have loved you with an everlasting love;
therefore I have continued my faithfulness to you.

JEREMIAH 31:3 NRSV

September 6

How beautiful on the mountains are the feet of those
who bring good news, who proclaim peace, who
bring good tidings, who proclaim salvation,
who say to Zion, "Your God reigns!"

ISAIAH 52:7 NIV

April 29

My purpose is that they may be encouraged in heart and united in love, so that they may have the full riches of complete understanding, in order that they may know the mystery of God, namely, Christ, in whom are hidden all the treasures of wisdom and knowledge.

Colossians 2:2–3 niv

September 5

Remember that at that time you were separate
from Christ. . .without hope and without God in the world.
But now in Christ Jesus you who once were far away have
been brought near through the blood of Christ.

EPHESIANS 2:12–13 NIV

April 30

For you created my inmost being; you knit me together
in my mother's womb. I praise you because I am
fearfully and wonderfully made; your works
are wonderful, I know that full well.

PSALM 139:13–14 NIV

September 4

"The LORD does not see as mortals see; they look on the
outward appearance, but the LORD looks on the heart."

1 SAMUEL 16:7 NRSV

May 1

For the earth shall be filled with the knowledge
of the glory of the LORD, as the waters cover the sea.

HABAKKUK 2:14 KJV

September 3

I have set the LORD always before me. Because he is at my right hand, I will not be shaken. Therefore my heart is glad and my tongue rejoices; my body also will rest secure.

PSALM 16:8–9 NIV

May 2

Come to me, all you that are weary and are carrying
heavy burdens, and I will give you rest. Take my yoke
upon you, and learn from me; for I am gentle and
humble in heart, and you will find rest for your souls.
For my yoke is easy, and my burden is light.

MATTHEW 11:28–30 NRSV

September 2

Love GOD, your God. Walk in his ways. Keep his
commandments, regulations, and rules so that you will live,
really live, live exuberantly, blessed by GOD, your God.

DEUTERONOMY 30:16 MSG

May 3

The heavens declare the glory of God; the skies proclaim the work of his hands. Day after day they pour forth speech; night after night they display knowledge.

PSALM 19:1–2 NIV

September 1

May the Lord continually bless you with
heaven's blessings as well as with human joys.

PSALM 128:5 TLB

May 4

"Forget the former things; do not dwell on the past.
See, I am doing a new thing! Now it springs up;
do you not perceive it? I am making a way in
the desert and streams in the wasteland."

ISAIAH 43:18–19 NIV

August 31

Now faith is being sure of what we hope for and certain of
what we do not see. . . . By faith we understand that
the universe was formed at God's command, so that what
is seen was not made out of what was visible.

HEBREWS 11:1, 3 NIV

May 5

GOD, your God, will outdo himself in making things
go well for you. . . . Yes, GOD will start enjoying
you again, making things go well for you just as
he enjoyed doing it for your ancestors.

DEUTERONOMY 30:9 MSG

August 30

"The LORD your God is with you, he is mighty to save.
He will take great delight in you, he will quiet you
with his love, he will rejoice over you with singing."

ZEPHANIAH 3:17 NIV

May 6

May the God who gives endurance and
encouragement give you a spirit of unity among
yourselves as you follow Christ Jesus.

ROMANS 15:5 NIV

August 29

Those who hope in the LORD will renew their strength.
They will soar on wings like eagles; they will run
and not grow weary, they will walk and not be faint.

ISAIAH 40:31 NIV

May 7

Reliable friends who do what they say are like
cool drinks in sweltering heat—refreshing!

PROVERBS 25:13 MSG

August 28

Search me, O God, and know my heart; test me and know
my anxious thoughts. See if there is any offensive way
in me, and lead me in the way everlasting.

PSALM 139:23–24 NIV

May 8

Your word, O LORD, is eternal; it stands firm in the heavens.
Your faithfulness continues through all generations;
you established the earth, and it endures.
Your laws endure to this day.

PSALM 119:89–91 NIV

August 27

The Sovereign LORD is my strength; he makes my feet like
the feet of a deer, he enables me to go on the heights.

HABAKKUK 3:19 NIV

May 9

An excellent wife, who can find? For her worth is far above jewels. . . . Her children rise up and bless her.

PROVERBS 31:10, 28 NASB

August 26

Is anyone thirsty? Come! All who will, come
and drink, drink freely of the Water of Life!

REVELATION 22:17 MSG

May 10

"May they who love you be like
the sun when it rises in its strength."

JUDGES 5:31 NIV

August 25

The LORD is my light and my salvation—whom
shall I fear? The LORD is the stronghold of
my life—of whom shall I be afraid?

PSALM 27:1 NIV

May 11

How precious to me are your thoughts, O God!
How vast is the sum of them! Were I to count
them, they would outnumber the grains of sand.

PSALM 139:17–18 NIV

August 24

And ye shall seek me, and find me, when ye shall search for me with all your heart. And I will be found of you, saith the LORD.

JEREMIAH 29:13–14 KJV

May 12

Let everything you say be good and helpful, so that your words will be an encouragement to those who hear them.

EPHESIANS 4:29 NLT

August 23

Now to him who by the power at work within us is able to
accomplish abundantly far more than all we can ask
or imagine, to him be glory in the church and in
Christ Jesus to all generations, forever and ever. Amen.

EPHESIANS 3:20–21 NRSV

May 13

The world of the generous gets larger and larger. . . .
The one who blesses others is abundantly
blessed; those who help others are helped.

PROVERBS 11:24–25 MSG

August 22

God is our refuge and strength, a very present help in trouble. Therefore will not we fear, though the earth be removed, and though the mountains be carried into the midst of the sea.

PSALM 46:1–2 KJV

May 14

Choose you this day whom ye will serve. . .but as for me and my house, we will serve the LORD.

JOSHUA 24:15 KJV

August 21

Blessed are they which are persecuted for
righteousness' sake: for theirs is the kingdom of heaven.

MATTHEW 5:10 KJV

May 15

The king is enthralled by your
beauty; honor him, for he is your lord.

PSALM 45:11 NIV

August 20

Then I looked, and I heard the voice of
many angels. . .singing with full voice,
"Worthy is the Lamb."

REVELATION 5:11–12 NRSV

May 16

I lay down and slept. I woke up in safety, for the LORD was watching over me. I am not afraid of ten thousand enemies who surround me on every side.

PSALM 3:5–6 NLT

August 19

It is you who light my lamp; the LORD, my God, lights up my darkness. By you I can crush a troop, and by my God I can leap over a wall.

PSALM 18:28–29 NRSV

May 17

Be devoted to one another in brotherly love.
Honor one another above yourselves.

ROMANS 12:10 NIV

August 18

In him we have redemption through his blood,
the forgiveness of sins, in accordance with the
riches of God's grace that he lavished on us
with all wisdom and understanding.

EPHESIANS 1:7–8 NIV

May 18

If. . .you seek the LORD your God, you will find him if you look for him with all your heart and with all your soul.

DEUTERONOMY 4:29 NIV

August 17

Our Father which art in heaven, Hallowed be thy name. Thy kingdom come. Thy will be done in earth, as it is in heaven. Give us this day our daily bread. And forgive us our debts, as we forgive our debtors. And lead us not into temptation, but deliver us from evil: For thine is the kingdom, and the power, and the glory, for ever. Amen.

MATTHEW 6:9–13 KJV

May 19

Be kind to one another, tenderhearted, forgiving
one another, as God in Christ has forgiven you.

EPHESIANS 4:32 NRSV

August 16

"So let us know, let us press on to know the LORD. His going forth is as certain as the dawn; and He will come to us like the rain, like the spring rain watering the earth."

HOSEA 6:3 NASB

May 20

So I tell you, whatever you ask for in prayer, believe
that you have received it, and it will be yours.

MARK 11:24 NRSV

August 15

One thing have I desired of the LORD, that will I seek after; that I may dwell in the house of the LORD all the days of my life, to behold the beauty of the LORD, and to enquire in his temple. For in the time of trouble he shall hide me in his pavilion: in the secret of his tabernacle shall he hide me; he shall set me up upon a rock.

PSALM 27:4–5 KJV

May 21

Hear my cry, O God; listen to my prayer. From the ends of the earth I call to you, I call as my heart grows faint; lead me to the rock that is higher than I. For you have been my refuge.

PSALM 61:1–3 NIV

God demonstrates His own love toward us, in that
while we were yet sinners, Christ died for us.

ROMANS 5:8 NASB

May 22

Bring ye all the tithes into the storehouse. . .and prove me now herewith, saith the LORD of hosts, if I will not open you the windows of heaven, and pour you out a blessing, that there shall not be room enough to receive it.

MALACHI 3:10 KJV

August 13

"But He knows the way I take; when He has
tried me, I shall come forth as gold."

JOB 23:10 NASB

May 23

In him we were also chosen, having been predestined
according to the plan of him who works out everything
in conformity with the purpose of his will, in order
that we, who were the first to hope in Christ,
might be for the praise of his glory.

EPHESIANS 1:11–12 NIV

August 12

I will lie down and sleep in peace, for you alone, O LORD, make me dwell in safety.

PSALM 4:8 NIV

May 24

The way Christ treats the church. . .provides a good picture of how each husband is to treat his wife, loving himself in loving her, and how each wife is to honor her husband.

EPHESIANS 5:32–33 MSG

August 11

But don't, dear friend, resent GOD's discipline; don't
sulk under his loving correction. It's the child he loves
that GOD corrects; a father's delight is behind all this.

PROVERBS 3:11–12 MSG

May 25

I will give them an undivided heart and put a new spirit in them; I will remove from them their heart of stone and give them a heart of flesh.

EZEKIEL 11:19 NIV

August 10

Be not forgetful to entertain strangers: for
thereby some have entertained angels unawares.

HEBREWS 13:2 KJV

May 26

Like apples of gold in settings of silver is a word spoken
in right circumstances. Like an earring of gold and an
ornament of fine gold is a wise reprover to a listening ear.

PROVERBS 25:11–12 NASB

August 9

I will repay you for the years the locusts have eaten. . . .
And you will praise the name of the LORD your
God, who has worked wonders for you.

JOEL 2:25–26 NIV

May 27

God's love is meteoric, his loyalty astronomic,
his purpose titanic, his verdicts oceanic.
Yet in his largeness nothing gets lost.

PSALM 36:5–6 MSG

August 8

Search high and low, scan skies and land, you'll find
nothing and no one quite like GOD. The holy angels
are in awe before him; he looms immense and august
over everyone around him. GOD. . .who is like
you, powerful and faithful from every angle?

PSALM 89:6–8 MSG

May 28

We also rejoice in our sufferings, because we know that
suffering produces perseverance; perseverance, character;
and character, hope. And hope does not disappoint us,
because God has poured out his love into our hearts
by the Holy Spirit, whom he has given us.

ROMANS 5:3–5 NIV

August 7

The promise of "arrival" and "rest" is still there for God's people. God himself is at rest. And at the end of the journey we'll surely rest with God. So let's keep at it and eventually arrive at the place of rest, not drop out through some sort of disobedience.

HEBREWS 4:9–11 MSG

May 29

Without faith it is impossible to please God, because anyone who comes to him must believe that he exists and that he rewards those who earnestly seek him.

HEBREWS 11:6 NIV

August 6

"No eye has seen, no ear has heard, no mind has conceived what God has prepared for those who love him."

1 Corinthians 2:9 niv

I will bless the L<small>ORD</small> at all times; his
praise shall continually be in my mouth.

P<small>SALM</small> 34:1 <small>NRSV</small>

August 5

GOD intended, out of the goodness of his heart, to be lavish in his revelation.

ISAIAH 42:21 MSG

May 31

He shall feed his flock like a shepherd: he shall gather the
lambs with his arm, and carry them in his bosom,
and shall gently lead those that are with young.

ISAIAH 40:11 KJV

August 4

"For I will pour water on the thirsty land, and streams on the dry ground; I will pour out my Spirit on your offspring, and my blessing on your descendants."

ISAIAH 44:3 NIV

June 1

The LORD will guide you always; he will satisfy your needs
in a sun-scorched land. . . . You will be like a well-watered
garden, like a spring whose waters never fail.

ISAIAH 58:11 NIV

August 3

Again Jesus spoke to them, saying, "I am the light of
the world. Whoever follows me will never walk
in darkness but will have the light of life."

JOHN 8:12 NRSV

June 2

For a day in thy courts is better than a thousand. I had rather be a doorkeeper in the house of my God, than to dwell in the tents of wickedness. For the LORD God is a sun and shield: the LORD will give grace and glory: no good thing will he withhold from them that walk uprightly.

PSALM 84:10–11 KJV

August 2

You who serve God, praise God! Just to speak his name
is praise! Just to remember God is a blessing—now
and tomorrow and always. From east to west, from dawn
to dusk, keep lifting all your praises to God!

PSALM 113:1–3 MSG

June 3

In the beginning was the Word, and the Word was with God, and the Word was God. He was in the beginning with God. All things came into being through him, and without him not one thing came into being. What has come into being in him was life, and the life was the light of all people.

JOHN 1:1–4 NRSV

August 1

"I am the LORD your God, who brought you
out of Egypt, out of the land of slavery.
You shall have no other gods before me."

EXODUS 20:2–3 NIV

June 4

I will send down showers in season;
there will be showers of blessing.

EZEKIEL 34:26 NIV

July 31

The Lord is faithful in all his words,
and gracious in all his deeds.

Psalm 145:13 NRSV

June 5

My help comes from the LORD, who made heaven and earth.
He. . .will neither slumber nor sleep. The LORD is your
keeper; the LORD is your shade at your right hand.

PSALM 121:2, 4–5 NRSV

July 30

Finally, be strong in the Lord and in his mighty power.
Put on the full armor of God so that you can take your
stand against the devil's schemes. For our struggle is not
against flesh and blood, but against the rulers, against
the authorities, against the powers of this dark world. . . .
Therefore put on the full armor of God, so that when
the day of evil comes, you may be able to stand your
ground, and after you have done everything, to stand.

EPHESIANS 6:10–13 NIV

June 6

I pray also that the eyes of your heart may be enlightened
in order that you may know the hope to which he has called
you, the riches of his glorious inheritance in the saints,
and his incomparably great power for us who believe.

EPHESIANS 1:18–19 NIV

July 29

When he saw the crowds, he had compassion on them,
because they were harassed and helpless, like
sheep without a shepherd. Then he said to his disciples,
"The harvest is plentiful but the workers are few.
Ask the Lord of the harvest, therefore, to send
out workers into his harvest field."

MATTHEW 9:36–38 NIV

June 7

"You're blessed when you're content with just who you are—no more, no less. That's the moment you find yourselves proud owners of everything that can't be bought. You're blessed when you've worked up a good appetite for God. He's food and drink in the best meal you'll ever eat."

MATTHEW 5:5–6 MSG

July 28

My command is this: Love each other as I have
loved you. Greater love has no one than this,
that he lay down his life for his friends.

JOHN 15:12–13 NIV

June 8

The LORD is good to everyone. He showers
compassion on all his creation.

July 27

Where can I go from your Spirit? Where can I flee from your presence? If I go up to the heavens, you are there; if I make my bed in the depths, you are there. If I rise on the wings of the dawn, if I settle on the far side of the sea, even there your hand will guide me, your right hand will hold me fast.

PSALM 139:7–10 NIV

June 9

But whatever was to my profit I now consider loss for the
sake of Christ. What is more, I consider everything a loss
compared to the surpassing greatness of knowing Christ
Jesus my Lord. . .that I may gain Christ and be found
in him, not having a righteousness of my own that comes
from the law, but that which is through faith in Christ.

PHILIPPIANS 3:7–9 NIV

July 26

I thank my God always concerning you, for the grace of
God which was given you in Christ Jesus, that in everything
you were enriched in Him, in all speech and all knowledge,
even as the testimony concerning Christ was confirmed
in you, so that you are not lacking in any gift, awaiting
eagerly the revelation of our Lord Jesus Christ.

1 CORINTHIANS 1:4–7 NASB

June 10

The first thing I want you to do is pray. Pray every way you know how, for everyone you know. Pray especially for rulers and their governments to rule well so we can be quietly about our business of living simply, in humble contemplation. This is the way our Savior God wants us to live.

1 TIMOTHY 2:1–3 MSG

July 25

Praise ye the LORD. Praise God in his sanctuary: praise him in the firmament of his power. Praise him for his mighty acts: praise him according to his excellent greatness. Let every thing that hath breath praise the LORD. Praise ye the LORD.

PSALM 150:1–2, 6 KJV

June 11

Yet I am always with you; you hold me by my right hand. You guide me with your counsel, and afterward you will take me into glory.

PSALM 73:23–24 NIV

July 24

For our light affliction, which is but for a moment, worketh for us a far more exceeding and eternal weight of glory.

2 Corinthians 4:17 kjv

June 12

"I will refresh the weary and satisfy the faint."

JEREMIAH 31:25 NIV

July 23

The LORD gives strength to his people; the
LORD blesses his people with peace.

PSALM 29:11 NIV

June 13

God does not respond to what we do; we respond to what
God does. We've finally figured it out. Our lives get in step
with God and all others by letting him set the pace,
not by proudly or anxiously trying to run the parade.

ROMANS 3:27–28 MSG

July 22

But each of us was given grace according
to the measure of Christ's gift.

EPHESIANS 4:7 NRSV

June 14

"Blessed be the LORD, who has given rest to His people Israel, according to all that He promised; not one word has failed of all His good promise."

1 KINGS 8:56 NASB

July 21

Happy are those who do not follow the advice of the wicked, or take the path that sinners tread, or sit in the seat of scoffers; but their delight is in the law of the LORD, and on his law they meditate day and night. They are like trees planted by streams of water, which yield their fruit in its season, and their leaves do not wither. In all that they do, they prosper.

PSALM 1:1–3 NRSV

June 15

"Do not be afraid. I am the First and the Last.
I am the Living One; I was dead, and
behold I am alive for ever and ever!"

REVELATION 1:18 NIV

July 20

You'll get a brand-new name straight from the mouth of GOD. You'll be a stunning crown in the palm of GOD's hand. . . . As a bridegroom is happy in his bride, so your God is happy with you.

ISAIAH 62:2–3, 5 MSG

June 16

Send forth your light and your truth, let them guide me;
let them bring me to your holy mountain, to the
place where you dwell. Then will I go to the altar of
God, to God, my joy and my delight.

PSALM 43:3–4 NIV

July 19

Ah LORD God! behold, thou hast made the heaven
and the earth by thy great power and stretched
out arm, and there is nothing too hard for thee.

JEREMIAH 32:17 KJV

Always be joyful. Keep on praying. No matter
what happens, always be thankful, for this is
God's will for you who belong to Christ Jesus.

1 THESSALONIANS 5:16–18 NLT

July 18

The eternal God is your refuge, and
underneath are the everlasting arms.

DEUTERONOMY 33:27 NIV

June 18

"God is one and there is no other. And loving him with all passion and intelligence and energy, and loving others as well as you love yourself. Why, that's better than all offerings and sacrifices put together!"

MARK 12:32–33 MSG

July 17

I pray that you, being rooted and established in love, may have power, together with all the saints, to grasp how wide and long and high and deep is the love of Christ, and to know this love that surpasses knowledge—that you may be filled to the measure of all the fullness of God.

EPHESIANS 3:17–19 NIV

June 19

What a God! His road stretches straight and smooth.
Every GOD-direction is road-tested. Everyone who
runs toward him makes it. Is there any god like GOD?

PSALM 18:30–31 MSG

July 16

Everything in the world is about to be wrapped up, so take nothing for granted. Stay wide-awake in prayer. Most of all, love each other as if your life depended on it. Love makes up for practically anything.

1 PETER 4:7–8 MSG

June 20

I truly delight in God's commands, but it's pretty obvious
that not all of me joins in that delight. Parts of me covertly
rebel, and just when I least expect it, they take charge.
I've tried everything and nothing helps. I'm at the end
of my rope. Is there no one who can do anything
for me? Isn't that the real question? The answer,
thank God, is that Jesus Christ can and does.

ROMANS 7:22–25 MSG

July 15

Many are saying to me, "There is no help for you in God." But you, O LORD, are a shield around me, my glory, and the one who lifts up my head. I cry aloud to the LORD, and he answers me from his holy hill.

PSALM 3:2–4 NRSV

June 21

Thank the LORD for his steadfast love, for his wonderful works to humankind. For he satisfies the thirsty, and the hungry he fills with good things.

PSALM 107:8–9 NRSV

July 14

In returning and rest shall ye be saved; in quietness
and in confidence shall be your strength.

ISAIAH 30:15 KJV

June 22

You will experience God's peace, which is far more wonderful than the human mind can understand. His peace will guard your hearts and minds as you live in Christ Jesus.

PHILIPPIANS 4:7 NLT

July 13

But let all who take refuge in you be glad; let them ever sing for joy. Spread your protection over them, that those who love your name may rejoice in you. For surely, O LORD, you bless the righteous; you surround them with your favor as with a shield.

PSALM 5:11–12 NIV

June 23

He himself bore our sins in his body on the cross, so that, free from sins, we might live for righteousness; by his wounds you have been healed.

1 PETER 2:24 NRSV

July 12

A glad heart makes a cheerful countenance. . . .
A cheerful heart has a continual feast.

PROVERBS 15:13, 15 NRSV

June 24

All your works shall give thanks to you, O Lord, and all your faithful shall bless you. They shall speak of the glory of your kingdom, and tell of your power, to make known to all people your mighty deeds, and the glorious splendor of your kingdom. Your kingdom is an everlasting kingdom, and your dominion endures throughout all generations.

PSALM 145:10–13 NRSV

July 11

For God so loved the world that he gave his one
and only Son, that whoever believes in him
shall not perish but have eternal life.

JOHN 3:16 NIV

June 25

Every good gift and every perfect gift is from above,
and cometh down from the Father of lights, with
whom is no variableness, neither shadow of turning.

JAMES 1:17 KJV

July 10

O sing to the L ORD a new song; sing to the L ORD, all the
earth. Sing to the L ORD, bless his name; tell of his salvation
from day to day. Declare his glory among the nations,
his marvelous works among all the peoples.

P SALM 96:1–3 NRSV

June 26

Who is a God like you, who pardons sin. . . ?
You do not stay angry forever but delight to show mercy.
You will again have compassion on us.

MICAH 7:18–19 NIV

July 9

At the time, discipline isn't much fun. It always feels like it's going against the grain. Later, of course, it pays off handsomely, for it's the well-trained who find themselves mature in their relationship with God.

HEBREWS 12:11 MSG

June 27

The secret things belong to the LORD our God, but the things revealed belong to us and to our children forever, that we may follow all the words of this law.

DEUTERONOMY 29:29 NIV

July 8

He made known to us the mystery of his will according to
his good pleasure, which he purposed in Christ,
to be put into effect when the times will have reached their
fulfillment—to bring all things in heaven and on earth
together under one head, even Christ.

EPHESIANS 1:9–10 NIV

June 28

Surprise us with love at daybreak; then we'll skip and dance all the day long. . . . Let your servants see what you're best at—the ways you rule and bless your children. And let the loveliness of our Lord, our God, rest on us, confirming the work that we do. Oh, yes. Affirm the work that we do!

PSALM 90:14, 16–17 MSG

July 7

I will lift up mine eyes unto the hills, from whence cometh my help. My help cometh from the LORD, which made heaven and earth.

PSALM 121:1–2 KJV

June 29

"I will be with you, and I will protect you wherever you go."

GENESIS 28:15 NLT

July 6

May God, who puts all things together, makes all things whole. . .who led Jesus, our Great Shepherd, up and alive from the dead, now put you together, provide you with everything you need to please him. . .by means of the sacrifice of Jesus, the Messiah. All glory to Jesus forever and always!

HEBREWS 13:20–21 MSG

June 30

But the path of the righteous is like the light of dawn,
that shines brighter and brighter until the full day.

PROVERBS 4:18 NASB

July 5

Peace I leave with you, my peace I give unto you: not as the world giveth, give I unto you. Let not your heart be troubled, neither let it be afraid.

JOHN 14:27 KJV

July 1

Blessed are the merciful, for they will be shown mercy.

MATTHEW 5:7 NIV

July 4

Blessed is the nation whose God is the LORD.

PSALM 33:12 NIV

July 2

May God himself, the God of peace, sanctify you through
and through. May your whole spirit, soul and body be
kept blameless at the coming of our Lord Jesus Christ.
The one who calls you is faithful and he will do it.

1 THESSALONIANS 5:23–24 NIV

July 3

Who shall separate us from the love of Christ? Shall trouble
or hardship or persecution or famine or nakedness or
danger or sword? . . . No, in all these things we are more
than conquerors through him who loved us.

ROMANS 8:35, 37 NIV